INSIDE OUT.

HOW TO EMPOWER AND EVOLVE YOUR LIFE

COMPANION
WORKBOOK

Printing in USA

Liberation's Publishing LLC
501 7th St. N Suite 4 Columbus, MS. 39701

ISBN: 978 1 960853 77 6

Table of Contents

Dear Reader,

Your journey to empowerment and evolution starts with one decision—choosing you. Life has a way of testing our resilience, but every challenge you face is an opportunity to grow, to break free from limitations, and to step fully into your purpose. This workbook isn't just about reading—it's about doing, reflecting, and transforming. The power to change your life isn't in the hands of anyone else. It's in yours. But real transformation requires commitment. You must be willing to show up for yourself every single day, even when it's hard, even when the progress seems slow, even when doubt tries to creep in. Growth isn't always easy, but neither is staying stuck. So, I encourage you—commit to the journey. Commit to becoming the best version of yourself, one intentional step at a time. Use these pages as your guide, your mirror, and your roadmap to unlocking everything that is already within you. You have the power to empower and evolve. The question is—are you ready to claim it? Let's do this together!

WITH LOVE AND PURPOSE.

Melissa

Chapter 01

The Decisions of Life

Reflection Questions:

What are some decisions from your past that shaped your current path?

_____
_____
_____
_____
_____
_____
_____
_____

How do you weigh the pros and cons of major decisions?

_____
_____
_____
_____
_____
_____
_____

I TRUST THE TIMING OF MY LIFE AND KNOW THAT EVERYTHING HAPPENS FOR A REASON.

Activity

Create a "Decision Map" for an upcoming choice. List possible outcomes, pros, and cons for each option.

Choice

Outcome

Outcome

Pro

Con

Pro

Con

The Weight of Living Out of Alignment

Reflection Questions:

What distractions are currently keeping you from your purpose?

_____
_____
_____
_____
_____
_____
_____
_____

Are there any "secrets" or burdens you're carrying that need to be addressed?

_____
_____
_____
_____
_____
_____
_____

I TRUST THAT EVERY SETBACK IS A SETUP FOR A COMEBACK.

Activity:

Write a letter to yourself identifying one step you'll take toward rediscovering your purpose.

Chapter

03

Turning Negative Thoughts into Positive Ones

Reflection Questions:

What are three recurring negative thoughts you've had recently?

_____

_____

_____

_____

_____

_____

_____

How can you reframe them into positive affirmations?

_____

_____

_____

_____

_____

_____

_____

I AM CONSTANTLY LEARNING AND GROWING.

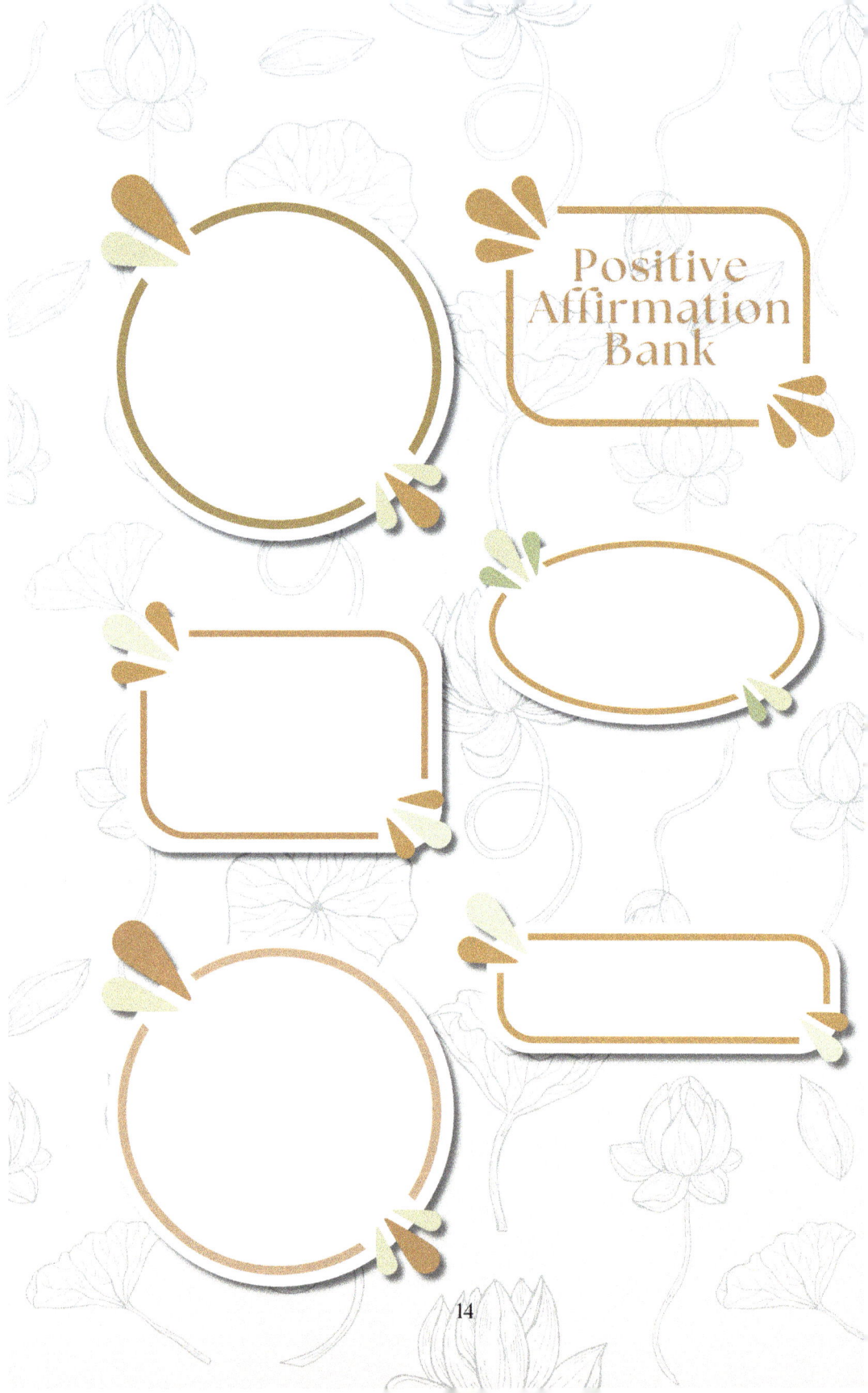

Positive
Affirmation
Bank

14

chapter

04

Stop Negotiating Disrespect: Know Your Worth

Reflection Questions:

In what areas of your life are you tolerating less than you deserve?

_____
_____
_____
_____
_____
_____
_____

What boundaries do you need to establish?

_____
_____
_____
_____
_____
_____

I AM PROUD
OF THE PERSON
I AM
BECOMING.

Respect Contract

This contract is made between me, myself and I as a declaration of my self-worth, personal boundaries, and commitment to being treated with the respect I deserve.

Section 1: My Non-Negotiables

I commit to ensuring that the following principles are upheld in all my relationships—personal, professional, and social. I will not tolerate any violation of these standards:

○ _____

○ _____

○ _____

○ _____

○ _____

○ _____

Section 2: My Commitments to Enforce This Contract

To honor myself, I commit to the following actions:

○ _____

○ _____

○ _____

○ _____

○ _____

○ _____

○ _____

○ _____

○ _____

○ _____

○ _____

○ _____

○ _____

○ _____

○ _____

By signing this contract, I
acknowledge that I am worthy of
respect and will not settle for
anything less. I honor and enforce
these commitments for my well-
being.

 *Signed:*

Chapter 05

Stop Ripping the Band-Aid Off: Stay Healed

Reflection Questions:

What unresolved wounds from your past still affect you?

_____

_____

_____

_____

_____

_____

_____

What steps have you taken toward healing, and what's still needed?

_____

_____

_____

_____

_____

_____

_____

I DESERVE TO BE HAPPY, HEALTHY, AND SUCCESSFUL

ACTIVITY:

Write out a plan for engaging in counseling, prayer, or other healing practices over the next 6 months.

Write it out		
Month 1	Month 2	Month 3

Write it out

Month 4	Month 5	Month 6

Chapter

06

Emotional
Intelligence

Reflection
Questions:

What emotions do you struggle to control, and why?

_____

_____

_____

_____

_____

_____

_____

_____

How do you respond to conflict?

_____

_____

_____

_____

_____

_____

_____

_____

I AM WORTHY OF
EVERYTHING I DESIRE
IN LIFE.

EMOTIONAL TRACKER

DAYS	TRIGGERS	EMOTIONS	MANAGE
S			
M			
T			
W			
T			
F			
S			

Activity: Keep an "Emotional Tracker" for one week, noting your triggers, emotions, and how you managed them.

Chapter

07

Pouring Into Others: Finding Your Purpose in Life

Reflection
Questions:

Who in your life could benefit from your wisdom or time?

_____

_____

_____

_____

_____

_____

_____

_____

How does helping others align with your purpose?

_____

_____

_____

_____

_____

_____

_____

I TRUST THAT
EVERY SETBACK IS
A SETUP FOR A
COMEBACK.

Purpose Plan

Activity: Create a "Purpose Plan" outlining ways you can serve and inspire others.

Purpose Plan

Activity: Create a "Purpose Plan" outlining
ways you can serve and inspire others.

41

Chapter

08

Learning to Be Still and Be Quiet in the Moment

Reflection
Questions:

How often do you spend quiet time with
God or yourself?

_____
_____
_____
_____
_____
_____
_____

What distractions prevent you from
being present in the moment?

_____
_____
_____
_____
_____
_____

I TRUST THAT I
AM EXACTLY
WHERE I NEED TO
BE IN THIS
MOMENT.

WRITE A MORNING PRAYER OR AFFIRMATION

Activity: Write a morning prayer or affirmation based on Psalms 5:3 to recite daily.

Psalms 5:3 says, "In the morning, O Lord, you hear my voice; in the morning I lay my requests before you and wait expectantly".

IMPORTANT

Chapter 09

Procrastination is NOT Your Friend

Reflection Questions:

What areas of your life are you procrastinating on?

_____
_____
_____
_____
_____
_____
_____

How does procrastination impact your emotional and physical health?

_____
_____
_____
_____
_____
_____
_____

I CHOOSE TO LET GO OF WHAT NO LONGER SERVES ME AND MAKE ROOM FOR GROWTH.

Weekly Goal Schedule

Activity: Create a detailed weekly schedule for one goal you've been putting off.

-DAY-	-TASK-	-PROGRESS-

Chapter

10

Being a Self-Thinker and a Self-Starter

Reflection Questions:

In what ways have you been authentically yourself?

_____

_____

_____

_____

_____

_____

_____

_____

How can you encourage independence and self-motivation in others?

_____

_____

_____

_____

_____

_____

_____

I RELEASE ALL NEGATIVITY AND EMBRACE POSITIVITY.

Activity:

Set three personal goals that showcase your individuality and autonomy.

Chapter

11

Grief

Reflection Questions:

What has grief taught you about yourself?

_____
_____
_____
_____
_____
_____
_____

How have you honored the memories
of loved ones you've lost?

_____
_____
_____
_____
_____
_____
_____

I TRUST THE
PROCESS OF LIFE
AND THE TIMING OF
MY GROWTH.

Activity:

Write a letter to a loved one you've lost, expressing your thoughts and emotions.

_____

_____

_____

_____

_____

_____

_____

_____

_____

_____

12

Self-
Reflection

Reflection
Questions:

What's one thing you've learned about
yourself through this workbook so far?

_____
_____
_____
_____
_____
_____
_____
_____

Are there areas where you've been
too hard on yourself?

_____
_____
_____
_____
_____
_____
_____

I AM IN CHARGE
OF HOW I FEEL,
AND TODAY I
CHOOSE
HAPPINESS.

Activity:

Take time to write a "Thank You"
letter to yourself for your progress
and growth.

_____

_____

_____

_____

_____

_____

_____

_____

_____

_____

_____

_____

_____

Chapter

13

The Power of Self-Reflection and Putting in the Work

Activity:

Question Bank:
Choose from the collection of open-ended questions to encourage deeper exploration of the themes from the book.

1. What values are most important to me right now?

2. How can I make decisions today that align with these values?

3. How can I shift my thoughts today to focus on positivity?

4. What is one thing I can do today to create a positive mindset?

5. What new opportunities am I facing right now?

6. How can I approach these opportunities with confidence?

7. In what areas do I need to give myself more grace?

8. How can I strive for excellence without being overly critical of myself?

9. How am I evolving, and what changes have I noticed?

10. What part of me do I want to focus on evolving this week?

Dear Empowered Reader,

You made it to the end of this workbook, but this is just the beginning of your journey. Every page you completed, every reflection you wrote, and every truth you faced was a step toward becoming the best version of yourself. Growth isn't always easy, but neither is staying the same. You've already proven that you are committed to evolving, and I want you to hold onto that strength. Remember this: You are worthy of every dream, every success, and every breakthrough. The only thing standing between where you are now and where you want to be is your commitment to keep going. Even on the hard days, even when doubt creeps in—keep choosing yourself. Keep pushing forward. Keep believing in what's possible for you.

I'm proud of you. I believe in you. And I can't wait to see how you continue to grow from the— inside out.

With gratitude and belief in you,

Melissa Richey-Bridges

Founder,
Empower and Evolve Solutions
Consulting

www.ingramcontent.com/pod-product-compliance
Lightning Source LLC
Chambersburg PA
CBHW051233120626

46547CB00013B/1629